EYEWITNESS DISASTER
VOLCANOES!

HELEN DWYER

 **Marshall Cavendish**
Benchmark
New York

This edition first published in 2011 in the United States of America
by MARSHALL CAVENDISH BENCHMARK
An imprint of Marshall Cavendish Corporation

Other Marshall Cavendish Offices:
Marshall Cavendish International (Asia) Private Limited, 1 New Industrial Road, Singapore 536196 • Marshall Cavendish International (Thailand) Co Ltd. 253 Asoke, 12th Flr, Sukhumvit 21 Road, Klongtoey Nua, Wattana, Bangkok 10110, Thailand • Marshall Cavendish (Malaysia) Sdn Bhd, Times Subang, Lot 46, Subang Hi-Tech Industrial Park, Batu Tiga, 40000 Shah Alam, Selangor Darul Ehsan, Malaysia

Marshall Cavendish is a trademark of Times Publishing Limited

Planned and produced by Discovery Books Ltd., 2 College Street, Ludlow, Shropshire, SY8 1AN www.discoverybooks.net
Managing editor: Rachel Tisdale
Editor: Helen Dwyer
Designer: sprout.uk.com Limited
Illustrator: Stefan Chabluk
Picture researcher: Tom Humphrey

Photo acknowledgments: Corbis: 7 (Frans Lanting), 17, 26 (Roger Ressmeyer), 29 (Reuters). Getty Images: 9 (Bruce Alexander/AFP), 10 (Philippe Bourseiller), 12 (Marco Longari/AFP), 13 (Pedro Ugarte/AFP), 14 (STF/AFP), 15 (Arlan Naeg), 16 (Richard Roscoe/Visuals), 17 (Roberto Campos/AFP), 19 (Astromujoff/The Image Bank), 25 (Science and Society Picture Library), 28 (Rodrigo Buendia/AFP). NASA: 21, 27. Shutterstock: cover (juliengrondin), 4 (Andrea Danti), 5 (juliengrondin), 8 (Sergio B), 11 (Bryan Busovicki), 23 (Katrina Leigh). Wikimedia: 15 (Mediacaster40), 18 (Donald A Swanson/USGS Cascades Volcano Observatory), 24 (Ranveig).
Cover Picture: Volcano erupting

Library of Congress Cataloging-in-Publication Data

Dwyer, Helen.
  Volcanoes / by Helen Dwyer.
    p. cm. -- (Eyewitness disaster)
  Includes bibliographical references and index.
  ISBN 978-1-60870-006-6
  1. Volcanoes--Juvenile literature. I. Title.
  QE521.3.D893 2010
  551.21--dc22
                          2009042150

Printed in China

CONTENTS

Words in **bold** or <u>underlined</u> are defined in the Glossary on page 30.

WHAT IS A VOLCANO?

A volcano is a hill or mountain, often conical-shaped, with an opening in the middle. The opening extends down into chambers of liquid rock deep inside Earth. This rock is called **magma**. It is less **dense** than solid rock and full of hot gases, so it rises up toward Earth's surface. When it reaches weak areas or cracks in the solid rock above it, the magma breaks through, or erupts.

In an active volcano, magma pushes up through weak points in Earth's rocks and then through the volcano mound itself. The mound is made of layers of material from previous eruptions.

"[The cloud looked] like a pine . . . for it rose to a great height on a sort of trunk and then split off into branches . . . Sometimes it looked white, sometimes blotched and dirty, according to the amount of soil and ashes it carried with it . . . On Mount Vesuvius broad sheets of fire and leaping flames blazed."

Pliny the Younger describes the eruption of Vesuvius, Italy, in 79 CE. This is the first written description of a volcanic eruption.

Magma

Volcanic ash, rocks, and lava from previous eruptions

Solid rock

When a volcano erupts, the liquid magma may flow down its sides, or it may explode into the air.

VOLCANO LEGENDS

The word *volcano* comes from a small island of that name off the coast of southern Italy. The ancient Romans believed it was the home of their blacksmith god Vulcan. They thought that the island's volcano was the chimney of Vulcan's workshop and that the volcano's eruptions were a sign that Vulcan was busy working.

The people of the Hawaiian Islands believed a goddess named Pele triggered volcanic eruptions by digging into the ground with a magic stick when she was angry.

In the twelfth century, a volcano called Hekla became active in Iceland. People in Europe believed that Hekla was the entrance to hell and that the lumps of **lava** that flew hissing through the air were the souls of people screaming in pain.

Eruption Patterns

Some volcanoes erupt regularly while others lie dormant (sleeping) for hundreds or even thousands of years. Volcanic eruptions are taking place all the time, but often they are in areas with few people, such as Alaska in North America or Siberia in eastern Russia. Fortunately, eruptions rarely cause large-scale human disasters.

WHERE CAN VOLCANOES BE FOUND?

Volcanoes only occur in certain places. The **crust**, Earth's outermost layer, is like a shell made up of lots of large, hard blocks that move about very slowly above a hotter, softer layer called the **mantle**. These blocks are called **tectonic plates**. Most volcanic activity takes place along plate edges, especially the area around the Pacific Ocean, which is known as the Pacific Ring of Fire.

Plate Movements

Some plate boundaries are pulling apart (diverging) from each other on the ocean floor. The space left as they separate is filled by magma that rises from below, then cools and hardens. The Mid-Atlantic Ridge, which runs from north to south through the Atlantic Ocean, is a divergent boundary with many volcanoes.

Other plate boundaries collide with each other (converge). Usually an oceanic plate is forced down (subducted) below a continental plate. As it is forced down to a depth of about 60 miles (100 kilometers) the oceanic plate starts to melt, forming new magma. This magma escapes through the crust, creating volcanoes on the edges of continents.

This world map shows how volcanoes (red dots) occur near or on tectonic plate edges (white lines). The pink band—where most volcanoes are located—covers an area known as the Pacific Ring of Fire. The blue band is the area known as the Mid-Atlantic Ridge, where plates are pulling apart. At its northern end are the volcanoes that formed Iceland. The gray arrows on the map show which way the larger plates are moving.

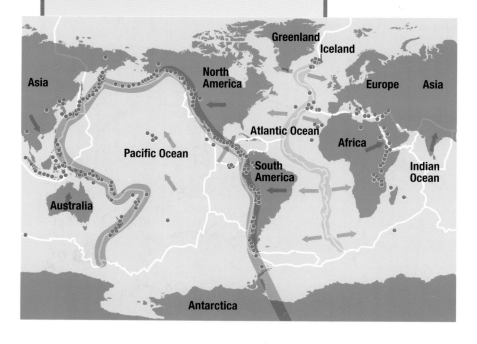

Greenland
Iceland
Asia
North America
Europe
Asia
Atlantic Ocean
Africa
Pacific Ocean
South America
Indian Ocean
Australia
Antarctica

The Galápagos Islands in the Pacific Ocean formed from volcanic activity above a column of hot rock called a mantle plume. As the tectonic plate moves above the plume, new volcanoes are formed. This photo shows volcanic craters on the island of Isabela.

RISING FROM THE SEA

New volcanoes are still being created in the oceans. In Hawaii, Lo'ihi Seamount began forming around 400,000 years ago. It has now risen 10,000 feet (3,000 meters) above the seafloor but it is not likely to break the ocean surface for at least 10,000 years.

In 1963 undersea volcanic eruptions created a new island called Surtsey, near the coast of Iceland. Surtsey continued to erupt and grow until 1967. Since then it has been worn away by the sea to an area of half a square mile (1.4 km²)—about half the size it was in 1967.

Hotspots

Some volcanoes occur away from plate boundaries in areas known as **hotspots**. These can be found above mantle plumes, which are columns of hot rock that rise through Earth's mantle and into the crust. The crust then melts, forming channels through which magma can escape. As the tectonic plates above move, the mantle plume stays in the same place. So, over millions of years, new volcanoes are formed and old ones become extinct. The Galápagos and Hawaiian islands were formed in this way.

TYPES OF ERUPTIONS

Red-hot lava flows from Mount Etna in Sicily. Etna is one of the most active volcanoes in the world, yet people still farm on the fertile soil at its base.

Volcanoes erupt in different ways. Eruptions can be gentle or explosive, depending on the sort of magma in the volcano. As magma rises, the gas bubbles inside it expand to hundreds of times their original size.

Types of Magma

If the magma is very runny liquid, the gases escape easily into the air, and the magma simply flows down the sides of the volcano. Once it is outside the volcano, this type of magma is known as lava.

If the magma is thick, the expanding gases are trapped. Eventually the pressure in the magma triggers an explosion as the gases force their way out. Magma is blasted into the air and breaks up into pieces. These fragments are called **tephra** and they range in size from small particles of ash to large boulders. Both lava and tephra become solid as they cool.

"The ash was mushrooming out in thick clouds ... [that] began to drift towards us.... The sky was darkening and black specks of ash were falling on us.... There was an overpowering smell of sulfur."

One eyewitness's experience of an eruption in Papua New Guinea, 1994.

Gas Dangers

The gases from a volcano can be as deadly as the lava and ash. They can poison people or animals nearby. If they rise high into the atmosphere they may mix with moisture to create **acid rain**, or they may block out heat and light from the Sun.

Pacific islanders watch from a safe distance as Tavurvur volcano sends clouds of ash over the town of Rabaul, Papua New Guinea, in 2006.

AMAZING ESCAPE

Inside an Ash Cloud

In 1982, Galunggung volcano in Indonesia erupted. About 90 miles (150 km) away, the crew and passengers on a British aircraft saw flashes of glowing light and the plane was filled with the smell of **sulfur dioxide**. The plane was enveloped in a volcanic ash cloud. Ash stuck to the engines and caused them to fail. The plane glided slowly downward—23,000 feet (7,000 m) in 16 minutes. Then, as ash broke off, the engines began to work again and the plane landed safely.

Following an Eruption

When hot volcanic material meets water, snow, or ice, it mixes with it to form mudslides. **Landslides** can also follow volcanic eruptions. Underwater eruptions sometimes cause shock waves called **tsunamis**, which spread out across the ocean and break as giant waves on coasts.

FLOWING LAVA

The volcanoes of Hawaii and Iceland are known as shield volcanoes because their low, curved shape resembles a shield. This shape is created by liquid lava flowing a long distance from the vent (opening) in all directions before it cools and turns to rock. The slopes of shield volcanoes are quite gentle, so the lava moves fairly slowly. Shield volcanoes generally do not have explosive eruptions. When they erupt they eject mainly molten lava. The lava can destroy property, but usually people have time to get out of its path.

Volcanoes on Hawaii

Hawaii's volcanoes are monitored around the clock, and people are rarely hurt by the erupting lava. Kilauea is the most active volcano in the world. It has been erupting regularly since 1983.

Lava and Ash

In other parts of the world, volcanoes produce a mixture of lava and more solid material and are made up of layers of lava, ash, and rocks. Mount Etna in Sicily is one of these. Lava from Etna often threatens villages on its slopes.

Lava Lakes

Very rarely, lakes of molten lava build up in the craters of volcanoes. Today there are

The top of this slow Hawaiian lava flow is beginning to cool and darken as it is exposed to the air. The lava underneath remains much hotter.

five lava lakes in the world. Two are in Africa's Great Rift Valley, where Earth's crust is pulling apart. One of these, Erta Ale in Ethiopia, has been erupting continuously since 1967.

"The incandescent [glowing] bubbling lava lake hisses like some badly burned porridge cauldron, overturning and occasionally belching molten lava."

Earth scientist Dougal Jerram, describing the lava lake in Erta Ale, Ethiopia.

Red-hot lava glows through a hole in a lava tube in Hawaii.

LAVA TUBES

Sometimes a stream of fluid lava cools and forms a crust on its top surface. Eventually the other surfaces may also cool to form a hollow tube. Liquid lava flows through this tube, but because it is surrounded by the newly solidified rock of the tube walls, its heat is trapped. The lava remains much hotter and more liquid—and also flows more quickly—than if it was exposed to the air. This makes it much more dangerous than ordinary lava, so sometimes people try to destroy lava tubes with explosives.

"All I see is burning trees and fire."

NYIRAGONGO, DEMOCRATIC REPUBLIC OF CONGO 2002

People in the city of Goma described the lava flows from Mount Nyiragongo:

"The ground started shaking and fire came out."
Furazh Kiza, Goma resident

"I've never seen so much fire in my life. I look up at the volcano and all I see is burning trees and fire."
Karine Morency, United Nations worker

"Most of the town has been . . . buried under thick, dense black mud [lava] which is hardening like concrete."
Alison Preston, aid worker

Mount Nyiragongo is Africa's most dangerous volcano. It was created by the African tectonic plate breaking apart. On January 17, 2002, a **fissure** opened up and spread 8 miles (13 km) down the volcano and across the plain to the edge of the city of Goma. Fountains of lava burst out along the fissure and a lava river—at times more than two-thirds of a mile (1 km) wide and 6.5 feet (2 m) high—spilled through the city, dividing it in two.

A young boy walks past smoking lava in Goma. About fifty people died from the poisonous gases coming from the lava.

Helping Hands

The tragedy in Goma left many people with burns that needed treatment. The **aid agency** Médecins Sans Frontières supplied burns kits to the hospital in Goma, which, fortunately, was unaffected by the lava. These kits contained bandages, **anesthetics** to relieve pain, **antibiotics** to prevent the burns becoming infected, and serum (a watery fluid) to help people who had become **dehydrated**.

Destruction in Goma

The people of Goma fled the lava as it destroyed their homes. The lava—and the earthquakes that followed—wrecked thousands of buildings and left 120,000 people homeless. Approximately one hundred people died in the disaster.

The Future

The volcano is still very active and scientists fear that the next eruption could be under the city itself. Even worse, it might be under nearby Lake Kiva, where it could set loose a cloud of poisonous gases—including **carbon dioxide** and **hydrogen sulfide**— that could kill millions of people.

"There is no water, no food, no shelter. Some people are feeling sick because of the smoke. Children are hungry."

Themis Hakizimana, photographer at Goma.

A gas station explodes in Goma after burning lava set fire to the gasoline.

RIVERS OF MUD

When ash and fragments of rock from a volcano mix with water, snow, or ice they sometimes create mudslides or landslides called **lahars**. This muddy mixture is very fluid so it can travel downhill at great speeds, but when it settles it becomes solid like cement. Volcanic mudslides kill many more people than lava does.

The Tragedy of Armero

In November 1985, the volcano Nevado del Ruiz erupted in Colombia. Hot ash and gas melted the snow and **glaciers** on the summit, creating several lahars that raced at nearly 40 miles per hour (60 kph) down into the river valleys on the volcano's sides.

"There was a lot of confusion. People were in shock. Hundreds of people were trapped. I could hear people screaming for help and then silence—an eerie silence."

A photographer described the scene three days after the mudslide in Armero, Colombia, 1985.

One of these lahars wiped out the riverside town of Armero. Eighty percent of the people died under the mud and almost all of the survivors were injured. Unfortunately, a storm had cut electricity to Armero, and radio broadcasts warning them the mudflow was coming never reached the people in the town.

Mount Pinatubo

In 1991, Mount Pinatubo erupted in the Philippines. Although this was the second largest eruption of the twentieth century, it had been predicted, so tens of thousands of people moved away from the area. Unfortunately, a major storm followed the eruption and rain mixed with the volcanic ash. The mudslides that followed killed 1,500 people.

The town of Armero, Colombia, was flooded with muddy water after mudslides from Nevado del Ruiz volcano struck without warning in 1985.

AMAZING ESCAPE

Saved by Chocolate

After Nevado del Ruiz volcano erupted and triggered the Armero mudslide, volunteers dug through the mud looking for survivors. For an entire week they rescued people from the mud, but after that there were no more signs of life. Then in early December, Red Cross workers noticed smoke coming from the rubble. They dug down to find 75-year-old Maria Rosa Echeverri, still in her house by her cooking fire. She had survived for twenty-four days on rice and chocolate.

Clouds of ash and steam erupt from Mount Pinatubo in 1991. The unexpected mudslides that followed proved to be more dangerous than the volcanic ash clouds.

ASH AND GAS FLOWS

One of the most deadly results of a volcanic eruption is a **pyroclastic flow**. This is a cloud of superhot ash, gases, and rocks that is ejected from a volcano. The cloud stays just above the ground and can travel downhill at more than 435 miles per hour (700 kph). Anyone caught in a pyroclastic flow will either be burned to death or will suffocate on the gases and ash.

Mount Vesuvius

The Roman cities of Pompeii and Herculaneum were destroyed by pyroclastic flows from Mount Vesuvius in 79 CE. In Herculaneum, which was closer to the volcano, people were burned to death.

Further away in Pompeii, the flow was not as hot but people there suffocated on the ash.

The Death of Saint-Pierre

The worst pyroclastic flow disaster in history occurred on the Caribbean island of Martinique in 1902. An eruption ripped open the top of Mount Pelée and a thick, black cloud of steam, gases, and ash was released. This pyroclastic flow was hotter than 1,830° F (1,000° C) and moved at a speed of 415 miles per hour (670 kph). In

This pyroclastic flow is from the volcano on the Caribbean island of Montserrat during an eruption in 2006.

seconds it had covered the city of Saint-Pierre, 4 miles (6.5 km) away. The city burned for many days. Of the population of 30,000, only two men survived.

> "I felt a terrible wind blowing, the earth began to tremble and the sky became suddenly dark. I ... felt my arms and legs burning."
>
> Léon Compère-Léandre, survivor of the Mount Pelée eruption, 1902.

AMAZING ESCAPE

The Man Who Lived Through Doomsday

The luckiest man in Saint-Pierre was in a windowless, underground prison cell when the volcano erupted. Louis Cyparis was waiting for breakfast when it suddenly grew very dark. Hot air mixed with fine ashes came through the barred window in the door and burned him. Cyparis jumped in agony in the cell and cried for help. He was found by rescuers four days later and set free. He joined an American circus as "The Man Who Lived Through Doomsday," sitting in a replica of his prison cell and telling visitors about his experience.

The streets of Esquel, Argentina, were covered in a thick layer of volcanic ash when Chaitén in Chile erupted in May 2008. People wore masks to avoid breathing in the ash.

"The whole north side of the summit crater began to move."

MOUNT SAINT HELENS MAY 1980

"The whole north side of the summit crater began to move. . . . The entire mass began to ripple and churn up."
Keith and Dorothy Soffel, flying over the volcano as it erupted

"It was just billowing . . . within [the] gray plume were white steam clouds, and there was lightning striking."
Valerie Pierson, forest ranger

"It was pitch black dark, the air was so thick with ash and smoke you couldn't see a foot in front of yourself. We were being pelted with what looked like huge globes of mud."
Jamie Walt, camper

Mount St. Helens is a volcano in the Cascade Mountains of Washington State. Since the middle of the nineteenth century, this snow-capped and forested mountain had been dormant. Then in early 1980 it began to stir. There were earthquakes and eruptions of steam. New craters formed and two fissures appeared on the north side. Most alarming of all, a bulge formed between the fissures and expanded outward by 6.5 feet (2 m) a day.

Ash from the Mount St. Helens eruption was blasted high into the atmosphere and eventually came down in eleven states.

This photo from above shows the damage caused on the north side of Mount St. Helens (top half of photo). The forests on this side of the volcano were destroyed in the eruption.

As the volcano erupted, hot ash, rocks, and gases flew out and flowed down the north side, overtaking the landslide.

Mudslides and Ash Clouds

The hot ash and gases melted snow and glaciers. The mixture of ash and water formed mudslides, which traveled 50 miles (80 km). At the same time, a column of ash escaped from the summit. In only fifteen minutes a mushroom-shaped ash cloud rose 15 miles (24 km) into the atmosphere. In all, the eruption killed fifty-seven people and destroyed more than two hundred houses.

Blasted Apart

On May 18, an enormous eruption blew apart the north side of the volcano where the bulge had been. The boulders and rock fragments created by the eruption became a landslide that covered an area of 23 square miles (60 km²).

ASH CHAOS

In Washington State, the ash was in the air for many days, causing temporary breathing problems for thousands of people. Ash blanketed many farms, destroying the crops, and covered roads and airports. The ash particles in the air made it very difficult to see. The ash also clogged and damaged engines, machines, and electrical equipment.

DEADLY POISONS

Volcanoes release a mixture of gases, which can have a major impact on people and the environment. For example, sulfur dioxide mixes with water to form acid rain. After an eruption, acid rain often falls on places downwind of the volcano.

Laki Erupts

In June 1783, Laki volcano in Iceland erupted, ejecting million of tons of **hydrogen fluoride** and sulfur dioxide. The hydrogen fluoride settled on plants and grass and was eaten by farm animals. The animals' joints became deformed so they could not walk, and their teeth grew uncontrollably. More than half the livestock in Iceland died. About a quarter of the human population died of either fluorine and sulfur dioxide poisoning or starvation.

"More poison fell from the sky than words can describe . . . The snouts, nostrils and feet of animals turned bright yellow and raw. All the earth's plants burned, withered and turned gray."

Jón Steingrímsson, parish priest near Laki, 1783–1784.

ICELAND
Laki volcano △

Laki erupts
June 8, 1783

Atlantic
Ocean

UNITED
KINGDOM
June 23

Bergen, Norway
June 10

St. Petersburg, Russia
June 26

Moscow, Russia
June 30

RUSSIA

Berlin, Germany
June 17

EUROPE
Paris, France
June 20

Prague, Czech Republic
June 16

Turin, Italy
June 20

Padua, Italy
June 20

Black
Sea

AFRICA

Mediterranean
Sea

Tripoli, Libya
June 30

Baghdad, Iraq
July 1

N
W E
S

500 miles
500 kilometers

Path of Laki's volcanic haze

This map shows how quickly the poisonous fog from Laki reached Europe, western Asia, and northern Africa. The fog lasted until October and was followed by a very cold winter.

The Laki Haze

Just days after Laki erupted, a sulfurous fog reached Europe. English poet William Cowper wrote: "(People) are indisposed by fevers . . . the labourers (are) carried out of the fields incapable of work and many die." Death records in Britain show thousands more people than usual died between August and October 1783.

> "The sun, at noon, looked as blank as a clouded moon and shed a rust-coloured light on the ground ... the heat was so intense that meat could hardly be eaten on the day after it was killed."
>
> *From the diary of British **naturalist** Gilbert White, summer 1783.*

Killer Carbon Dioxide

Carbon dioxide gas can be a killer, too. Lake Nyos in Cameroon, in western Africa, lies on the side of a volcano. Magma beneath the lake gives off carbon dioxide, which leaks into the water. In 1986 a large cloud of carbon dioxide was suddenly released from the lake. It rolled down two nearby valleys, suffocating 1,700 people.

HAWAIIAN VOG

Today in Hawaii, Kilauea volcano often releases sulfur dioxide. When the gas forms particles in the air it creates a haze that the islanders call vog—short for "volcanic smog." People nearby suffer from breathing problems such as bronchitis (lung inflammation).

A photo, taken from a space shuttle, shows a volcanic haze over the Hawaiian Islands.

GOING GLOBAL

There is plenty of evidence to show that a single volcanic eruption can affect Earth's climate. For example, the largest volcanic eruption ever recorded was from Mount Tambora in Indonesia in April 1815. The gases and ash from Tambora reached a height of 27 miles (43 km). Winds spread the ash particles around the world.

The Year Without a Summer

The eruption led to the following year, 1816, being known as "the year without a summer." In North America, northern Europe, and China, there were frosts and snowstorms in May and June. Crops throughout North American, Europe, and Asia were ruined. Thousands of people starved or were so weakened that they died from disease **epidemics**.

"Ground frozen hard, and squalls of snow ... icicles 12 inches long in the shade at noon day."

From the June 7, 1816, weather records of Edward Holyoke in New Hampshire.

This map highlights the worldwide effects of the Tambora eruption in 1816. Temperatures everywhere were lower than normal, especially in the northern continents.

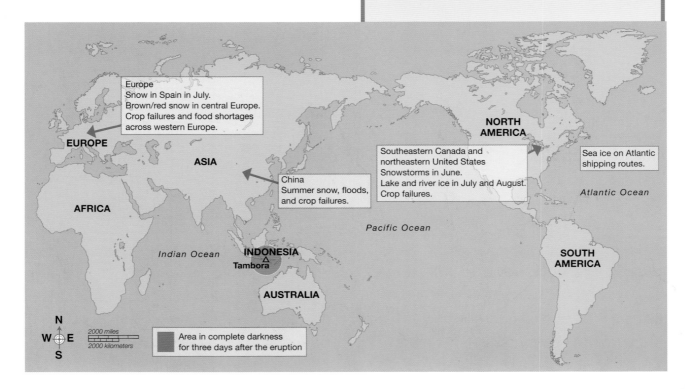

Europe
Snow in Spain in July.
Brown/red snow in central Europe.
Crop failures and food shortages across western Europe.

EUROPE

ASIA

AFRICA

China
Summer snow, floods, and crop failures.

NORTH AMERICA

Southeastern Canada and northeastern United States
Snowstorms in June.
Lake and river ice in July and August.
Crop failures.

Sea ice on Atlantic shipping routes.

Atlantic Ocean

Pacific Ocean

Indian Ocean

INDONESIA
△
Tambora

SOUTH AMERICA

AUSTRALIA

N
W ⊕ E
S

2000 miles
2000 kilometers

Area in complete darkness for three days after the eruption

In Yellowstone National Park, visitors can witness the effects of the high underground temperatures. Geysers (hot springs shooting out steam) erupt daily and mud boils in mud pots.

YELLOWSTONE CALDERA

Yellowstone National Park in Wyoming was the scene of a supervolcano eruption 640,000 years ago. When the magma chamber emptied, the land above it collapsed into the space the magma left. This type of land feature is called a **caldera**.

If there were to be another Yellowstone eruption of a similar size to the last one, most of North America would be covered with ash, the world's climate would be affected, and people would be unable to grow enough food. However, the scientists who study Yellowstone do not see any sign of that happening at the moment.

Supervolcanoes

Eruptions like Tambora do not occur very often, at most once every one or two thousand years. However, scientists have found evidence of much bigger volcanic eruptions in the past. They believe that there have been four **supervolcanoes**— ten times the size of Tambora—in the last million years. For example, about 75,000 years ago, ash from a volcano in Indonesia caused a global winter that lasted for a thousand years and killed most of the people on Earth. Now scientists are studying the world's volcanoes to find out where the next supereruption will take place.

23

"The wind . . . was hot and choking."

KRAKATOA, INDONESIA AUGUST 26–27, 1883

Many people aboard ships near Krakatoa later described their experiences:

" "[Krakatoa] became visible. Chains of fire appeared to ascend and descend between it and the sky. The wind . . . was hot and choking . . . with a smell as of burning cinders [ash]."
Captain Watson on a British ship

"A dense rain of mud fell . . . which made breathing difficult . . . the devilish smell of sulfurous acid spread. Some felt buzzing in the ears, others felt a pressing on the chest and sleepiness. It would have been quite natural if we had all choked to death."
N. H. van Sandick, passenger on a ship nearby "

Krakatoa was a small island in the Sunda Strait between the much larger islands of Sumatra and Java (part of Indonesia today). In 1883 it erupted with such violence that the explosions were heard in Australia, about 1,900 miles (3,000 km) away. Shock waves traveled through the air and circled Earth several times.

This 1888 illustration of Krakatoa is based on eyewitness reports of the eruption.

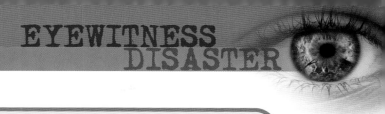

AMAZING ESCAPE

Tragedy in Sumatra

When Krakatoa erupted, the Beyerinck family was living in the coastal village of Ketimbang in Sumatra—25 miles (40 km) across the sea from the volcano. A tsunami struck the village and damaged their house. The family fled to their hillside hut but it was not as safe as they had hoped: a pyroclastic flow surged toward them over the sea from Krakatoa. The hut was in its path and fountains of hot ash spurted through the floorboards. The Beyerincks were badly burned and their baby died. Somehow they staggered back to the shore, where they found that all the villages had been swept away in another tsunami. The family was eventually rescued by a passing ship and taken to a hospital.

The Power of Tsunamis

Pyroclastic flows and showers of hot ash killed many people, but tsunamis proved to be even more deadly. These 18.5-foot-high (30-m) ocean waves were triggered by the pyroclastic flows, which dumped heavy rocks into the sea. The lighter materials and gases were carried on a layer of steam across the ocean to Sumatra, where pyroclastic flows probably killed more than 1,000 people. The tsunamis submerged many small islands, destroyed hundreds of coastal villages in Java and Sumatra, and caused the deaths of at least 35,000 people.

PREDICTING ERUPTIONS

Before scientists can predict a volcanic eruption, they need to know what is happening inside the volcano and recognize the events that come before an eruption. They gather this information in several ways.

Taking Measurements

Measuring gases is one way. Increases in sulfur dioxide emissions indicate rising magma. If increased emissions are followed by a decline in sulfur dioxide levels, a blockage might build up pressure in the magma and lead to an explosion.

Changes in the shape of the ground also show that magma is rising. These changes are measured by electronic devices and by comparing **satellite** images. Satellites also produce images that show changes in the heat inside a volcano.

Volcanologists (scientists who study volcanoes) collect gas samples from an opening near the crater rim of Colima volcano in Mexico.

Eruption Warnings

Volcanic activity is now carefully monitored by the Montserrat Volcano Observatory. The information it gathers is used to set changing danger levels for different regions of the island. People are advised not to enter areas where they might be in danger.

"Seeing how all the information ties in with each other, this gives us a detailed picture of what is happening and lets us forecast what is likely in the next hours, days and months."

Richard Robertson, director of the Montserrat Volcano Observatory, talking about the information gathered by the observatory.

A volcanologist checks ground movements recorded on a seismograph at Clark Air Base near the active Pinatubo volcano in the Philippines in 1991.

GLOSSARY

acid rain Rain made acidic by mixing with sulfur or nitrogen in the air; it is harmful to plants.

aid agency An organization that hands out supplies in emergencies.

anesthetics Medicines that stop any feeling of pain.

antibiotics Medicines that kill bacteria.

caldera A landscape feature created when land collapses in a volcanic eruption.

carbon dioxide A gas that is poisonous in large quantities and that is absorbed by plants.

crust The outermost solid layer of Earth, between 3 and 30 miles (5 and 50 km) thick.

dehydrated Having lost too much fluid.

dense Tightly packed.

epidemics Diseases affecting many people in the same region at the same time.

fissure A crack where rocks have split apart.

geological Concerning the study of Earth's rocks.

glaciers Slow-moving masses of ice that form from layers of crushed snow.

hotspots Places on Earth's surface above a mantle plume where volcanic activity occurs regularly.

hydrogen fluoride A very poisonous gas that damages the lungs and causes bone and tooth damage.

hydrogen sulfide A very poisonous gas that is especially dangerous to the nervous system in humans.

lahars Mudflows composed of volcanic ash, rocks, and water.

landslides Fast-moving masses of rock, soil, and debris.

lava Liquid rock after it has left a volcano.

magma Liquid rock beneath the surface of Earth.

mantle The mainly solid layer of Earth beneath the crust and above the core; it is nearly 2,000 miles (3,000 km) thick.

naturalist Someone who studies plants and animals.

pyroclastic flow A cloud of ash, rocks, and gas that erupts from a volcano and flows downhill close to the ground at high speeds.

satellite An unmanned object in orbit around Earth.

sulfur dioxide A gas that smells like rotten eggs, causes acid rain, and makes breathing difficult.

supervolcano A massive volcanic eruption that ejects at least 240 cubic miles (1,000 km^3) of material.

tectonic plates The segments that make up Earth's crust and upper mantle; they move around independently creating volcanoes and causing earthquakes.

tephra Fragments of magma ejected from a volcano in an explosive eruption.

tsunamis Huge waves caused by earthquakes, volcanoes, or landslides.

FURTHER INFORMATION

Books

Green, Jen. *Understanding Volcanoes and Earthquakes.* Our Earth. New York: Rosen, 2008.

Rubin, Ken. *Volcanoes and Earthquakes.* Insiders. New York: Simon & Schuster, 2007.

Townsend, John. *Earthquakes and Volcanoes: A Survival Guide.* Chicago: Heinemann, 2006.

Woods, Michael and Mary B. *Volcanoes.* Disasters Up Close. Minneapolis, MN: Lerner, 2007.

Websites

http://earthobservatory.nasa.gov/NaturalHazards/
NASA's website has lots of satellite images of volcanoes. You can see what an eruption looks like from space!

www.fema.gov/kids/volcano.htm
This website about volcanoes is made just for kids. Find volcano facts, learn how to map lava, find information about Mount St. Helens, and discover how vulcanologists measure volcanic explosivity.

http://kids.discovery.com/games/pompeii/pompeii.html
At *Discovery Kids*'s website, learn about tectonic plates and different types of volcanoes. You can take a look inside a volcano or even find directions to build your own volcano.

www.nationalgeographic.com/eye/volcanoes/volcanoes.html
This site includes information on volcanic effects and phenomena, interviews on Montserrat, videos of Mount St. Helens, and information on predicting volcanoes.

www.weatherwizkids.com/volcano1.htm
This website is designed by a TV meteorologist. It explains how a volcano erupts, the difference between magma and lava, plate tectonics, and much more!

INDEX
Page numbers in **bold** are photographs or diagrams